WOOD CARVING

BEING

A CAREFULLY GRADUATED EDUCATIONAL

COURSE FOR SCHOOLS AND ADULT CLASSES

By

JOSEPH PHILLIPS

1896

The Toolemera Press
History Preserved

www.toolemera.com

WOOD CARVING
by Joseph Phillips
Chapman And Hall, Ld.: London
1896

No part of this book may be reproduced, stored in an electronic retrieval system, or transmitted in any form or by an means, electronic, mechanical, photocopy, photographic or otherwise without the written permission of the publisher.

Excerpts of one page or less for the purposes of review and comment are permissible.

Copyright © 2013 The Toolemera Press
All rights reserved.

International Standard Book Number
ISBN : 978-0-9831500-8-4
(Trade Paperback)

Published by
The Toolemera Press
Massachusetts, U.S.A.

www.toolemera.com

Manufactured in the United States of America

More Reprints From Toolemera

- Mechanick Exercises, 1703 by Joseph Moxon
- The Mechanic's Companion, 1850 by Peter Nicholson
- The Circle Of The Mechanical Arts, 1813 by Thomas Martin
- Woodwork Tools And How To Use Them, 1922 by William Fairham
- Woodwork Joints, 1920 by William Fairham
- Cabinet Construction, 1930 by J. C. S. Brough
- Furniture Making: Advanced Projects In Woodwork, 1912 by Ira Griffith
- The Painter, Gilder, And Varnisher's Companion, 1850 by H. C. Baird
- Our Workshop, 1866 by Temple Thorold
- Carpentry And Joinery For Amateurs, 1879 by James Lukin
- The Art Of Mitring, 1892 by Owen Maginnis
- Working Drawings Of Colonial Furniture, 1912, F. J. Bryant

www.shop.toolemera.com

Toolemera Press Facsimile Editions

The Toolemera Press reprints classic books and ephemera on early crafts, trades and industries. We reprint titles held in our personal library. The Toolemera Press manages every aspect of the publishing process. All imaging is accomplished either in-house or by contract with respected document imaging services. We use Print-On-Demand to keep pricing affordable.

www.shop.toolemera.com

WOOD CARVING

WOOD CARVING

BEING

*A CAREFULLY GRADUATED EDUCATIONAL COURSE
FOR SCHOOLS AND ADULT CLASSES*

BY

JOSEPH PHILLIPS (MEDALLIST)

INSTRUCTOR OF WOOD CARVING, MODELLING, AND OTHER ART SUBJECTS
IN CONNECTION WITH VARIOUS CLASSES IN THE COUNTIES OF
LANCASHIRE, CHESHIRE, CUMBERLAND, AND NOTTS

*Approved by the Design Committee of the Home Arts and Industries
Association, Royal Albert Hall, London; Accepted as their
Scheme of Wood Carving by the Educational Handwork Union,
and by the Union of Lancashire and Cheshire Institutes*

LONDON: CHAPMAN AND HALL, Ld.

1896

INTRODUCTION

WOOD-CARVING as an educational influence appears to be entirely ignored, perhaps in consequence of its apparent limitations, both as to material used and manual exercises involved.

That it has such a value is undoubted, but as generally taught it simply amounts to keeping students employed, and as a consequence its educational value is seldom realised, because the student too frequently has no practical object in view. He may become skilful in the manipulation of tools and material if sufficiently persevering, but the realisation of an end and aim in his work may not dawn upon him whilst acquiring that technical skill.

The art of carving does not consist entirely in producing evidence of mastery over tools and material: this dexterity merely constitutes the means to an end; therefore to elucidate the principles underlying all good work would appear the most rational way to approach the subject.

What is wood-carving as distinguished from the art of wood-cutting? It is, or should be, one of the many means of expression. In this sense it is the expression in material form of ideas, the outcome of personal observation of nature and works done in ancient and modern times, or what we may see through the eyes of our favourite sculptor, etc., in which case we unfortunately surrender our own individualism.

It naturally follows that whatever influence affects the worker's mind must necessarily affect its expression; and thus we have in the carvings of past ages reflections in the concrete of people working in various climes and in different states of civilization, so that if it were necessary for the purpose of this book, there would be little, if any, difficulty in tracing minutely, character during the various periods of history.

Briefly stated, the material and its manipulation by different workers in the past ages may be regarded as a compound expression of character: in the cold, grey, would-be imperishable granite they used, and in its equally firm, severe, and unsympathetic treatment, may be found a basis for much conjecture as to the nature of the Egyptians; in the pure marble and its treatment, which requires a delicacy of touch, with a full appreciation of its nature, to bring out all its natural beauty, may be seen a clear reflection of the refinement of the Greeks as expressed in all they thought and did.

Brick and its limitation sufficed for early victorious Rome until an artificial refinement demanded marble. Money could and did supply this in abundance, but it was never stamped with anything but the characteristics of the people, as historically known.

Passing over the intervening space of time, we find in this country that wood, free-cutting stone, and its freer rendering, is still more clearly stamped with character, and may be classified as follows:

Norman Period—as Copper.

   Transitional.—Intermingling of a refining influence—Silver.

Early English.—Pure Silver.

   Transitional.—Fusion of gold into the silver.

Decorated.—Gold, the golden period, culminating in excess.

Perpendicular.—Mixture, deteriorating into dross, demonstrating the lamentable fact that the people had ceased to think for themselves, and so the work lost its charm.

On a further examination of the subject, it will be found that carving is an applied art—a building or article made more decorative, more interesting, by its application, and as such becomes part of a general scheme termed "Architecture": possibly a small part, but still an important one; and as the individual is to the nation, so is carving to architecture—the smallest things often speaking loudest of power, etc.

Understood, then, as a means of expression, it is therefore conducive to mental development, and carving may claim to be educational only when taught as such; *i.e.* the creation of visible evidence in material form of thought, however influenced.

This demand upon the creative faculty common to all, becomes a direct appeal for mental development, and the power of concentrating thought is thereby cultivated.

The sculptor may see in every block of stone a single figure, or group of figures, but it is the concentration of thought upon the group in his mind's eye that enables him to remove the superfluous stone, unfolding to view the hidden evidence or concrete reflection of his imagination.

Michael Angelo said that the object of sculpture was "to let out the angel."

Carving may take a prominent place as a branch of hand and eye training. In the former, accuracy and precision; through the latter, artistic power, refinement, appreciation of the beautiful in nature, may be cultivated and developed.

To qualify this generalising term, "go to nature." It would be well to ask what there is to admire in nature for our purpose. Firstly, beauty of form; this being improved by the addition of colour. Secondly, beauty of outline, whether seen in mass or detail. For instance, take an ivy leaf, and ask wherein is its beauty. Surely not altogether in that which may be seen at a first glance.

Few indeed are the instances where nature offers no reward for closer study than the passing glance. The first feature generally noticed is the outline, the stem, veins, etc.; but press the leaf in a book, and those features will still remain as a better example of technical skill than it is possible to produce in any other material.

Would this pressed leaf satisfactorily appeal to our intuitive ideals of its general appearance? No; because a void has been created, a something is absent; the pressure has robbed it of its beauty, its spirit, its life; the graceful form has departed, and all the wonderfully minute details fail to clothe the remaining skeleton of flatness; "it is uninteresting."

Seen, then, from this point of view, we cannot fail to appreciate the actual value of details; the technique, becoming monotonous as it approaches perfection, is by no means all, seeing that a leaf may be beautiful without the clear outline, stem, etc., whilst the same cannot be claimed for the pressed leaf.

Thus the creation of beautiful forms emphasised by details, *must* be the basis of all good work, the latter being relegated to a secondary position.

THE OBJECT OF THE BOOK.

To teach carving is the least, even if it be one, of the objects attempted. It is issued to fill a long-felt want for a graduated course of exercises, these being suggested by a long and varied professional and teaching experience — a course that shall be at once practical, and calculated to inculcate, though to a limited extent, the principles evolved from a careful study of nature and good works; these principles being the basis of every, and not the monopoly of any, particular style of carving, as Gothic, etc., which are but phases in the abstract life of ornament. The necessary expense of tools being an important matter, the most useful curves have been selected, and the first four plates may be worked with tools 1, 2, 3, 5; with one of No. 7 between three students, the complete course with 8, as given under the heading of tools, etc.

As a working motive such an outline is used, and, as careful observation will show, is the abstract form underlying natural leaves, either when complete as in the laurel, compound in the ivy, grouped in the rose, conventionalized in the acanthus.

The series of exercises also form the logical sequence of an attempt to develop by easy stages principles of design, as follows :—

Fig. 1. treats upon the technical side of the subject, the importance of which is apt to be overrated; for if the imaginative faculty is not being developed, there is little, if any, good purpose served by becoming proficient in the means of its expression.

The actual idea expressed by the grounding-out process is, that at given points the material not being required, is cut away.

Fig. II. must be an attempt to create a form more pleasing than the flat Fig. I.; and according to the appreciation of the beautiful in form, so the degree of success must be gauged.

Fig. III. is the application of the important principle of continuity of thought in line and mass.

Fig. IV. is the complete development.

Figs. VI., VII. is the application of this form of creative power, at any given place, to produce a desired result.

The leaf form Fig. I. is cut off at the point, and the square end turned under and over like a roll of paper.

Figs. IX., XI., similar forms to Fig. II., but treatments with different tools.

Figs. X., XII., similar forms to Fig. II., but

treatments with different tools, both upon the surface and outline. An exercise in relative value of tool-cuts : Figs. IX. and XI. are executed with tools 1 and 2, and Figs. X., XII., the same cuts emphasised with tool 2.

Figs. XIII.–XV., group of details Fig. I. An exercise in concentration of thought upon a given part in any arrangement of design. In this instance first the centre leaf.

Figs. XVI., XVII., a scroll.

Figs. XVIII., XIX., a scroll, with additions for space-filling purposes.

Figs. XX.–XXII., the same as Figs. XIII.–XV., but detail Figs. VI. and VIII. used instead of Fig. I.

Figs. XXIII., XXIV., useful details.

Figs. XXV., XXVI., the interlacing of stems in design. Fig. XXV. is a soulless rendering of Fig. XXVI. ; the latter is the application of principle inculcated in Fig. II.

Figs. XXVII.–XXX., the clothing of stems at their juncture with each other, etc.

Fig. XXXI., a design whose main stem is Fig. XVIII. enlarged, and clothed with details Figs. XXVII., XXIX., XXX.; also an exercise in confining the work within a border, thus preparing it for application to furniture, etc.

Fig. XXXII., a design containing useful details for future use.

Fig. XXXIII., a design with main stem Fig. XXVI., and details XXIII., XXIV., XXVII., XXIX.

Fig. XXXIV., a more decorative treatment of Figs. IX., XII. The edges are broken up.

Fig. XXXV., a more decorative treatment of Figs. IX., XII.

Fig. XXXVI., the grouping of details Figs. VI., VIII., XXVI.

Fig. XXXVII., the grouping of details Figs. XXXIV. and XXXV.

Fig. XXXVIII., based upon, and freer rendering of design Fig. XXXI.

If two are placed together an oblong panel is formed.

Fig. XXXIX., design similar to Fig. XXXVIII., but built up of details Fig. I., elaborated as Figs. XXXIV.–VII.

Fig. XL., the development of Fig. XXXVIII.

Each exercise has a distinct purpose, and the student cannot be too strongly advised to master each step, asking the reason of every peculiarity he may have noticed; and so being quite clear, he may go on, feeling assured of success—the secret of which is the combination of head and hand, the cultivation or recognition of a purpose at every stage of the work.

Each cut should be one towards the production of a fixed idea, although he

INTRODUCTION. 19

should always be ready to modify any such purpose if occasion presents itself.

To prevent the natural inclinations for "niggling" and hesitancy on the part of the student, large tools, and bold, vigorous strokes have been employed; in the cleaning of wood out of the corners, it is not so much a matter of using small tools as it is of cutting the wood properly down, when the large tool will jump the troublesome bit out. Too often the student will not do this, but, proceeding to drag it out, wonders why the corners remain so untidy. The apparent sameness of design is the outcome of compounding the first step throughout, and restriction in the number of tools.

A strictly limited edition of a similar scheme will be issued, in which natural details have been employed to express the same ideas; but as working to nature is attempting an unattainable standard, anything short of this standard may be counted "failure." How many workers have given up in despair because they discovered their inability to attain to the standard so foolishly fixed in their minds' eye, trying to carve like nature!

Most of the examples of such attempts are what may be termed caricatures of the original; and if not caricatures, then conventional treatments. If the latter, why not admit it, and derive the pleasure—"the fun" of twisting and fighting the material—with one object in view, that of producing beautiful forms and lines? That it is fascinating, who will deny?

The student working with fear and trembling, ever asking, Is this right? What must I do next? therefore ever dependent upon his teacher, etc., is more to be pitied than blamed.

Individual effort, however crude, is preferable to slavish attention to the material and its treatment, instead of the thoughts it is but the medium for expressing.

The author is prepared to introduce his scheme by bench lectures, with practical demonstration, to report upon work submitted, and pay periodical visits where desired.

In submitting his scheme he is not unmindful of its shortcomings, and any suggestions calculated to render the course still more useful will be appreciated.

TOOLS

THE full course has been worked out with the first eight tools on list, and called the "Ambleside set." The Sloyd Tool Co., Carver Street, Sheffield, supply this set as one of their many reliable specialities; few in number being the most desirable, as less to become acquainted with, so their possibilities for use the sooner discovered. Usually called gouges and chisels, of different curvatures and widths. No. 5 is a gouge, yet its curvature is sufficiently slight as to permit of its use as a chisel, thus serving the double purpose of gouge and chisel.

The sharpening of tools is a very important part of the work, and the process they undergo before being ready for use is grinding, whetting, and stropping. The former is done on a grindstone, which quickly removes the thick material usually on a new tool, in preparation for more careful treatment in the sharpening upon an ordinary joiner's oilstone, which removes any roughness that may be produced by the severe treatment on the grindstone. Carvers' tools are rubbed on both sides, not as joiners' tools. The treatment upon both sides gives a slight lever movement in cutting, thus enabling the tool to follow more easily the varying planes; the outside done on the oilstone by holding the tool nearly flat upon the face of the stone and at right angles, working it sideways from end to end of the stone; thus the curve of the tool will come in contact with the stone if the former is turned from corner to corner in the distance.

To make the figure 8 on the oilstone has been suggested, but the curves at the end of the figure allow the corners of the tool more than their share of friction, resulting in their being rounded too much. The inner sides of the gouges are rubbed by means of finger-slips, or small pieces of stone with curved edges. Olive or neat's-foot oil may be used. The principal thing to avoid is making the edges of the tools dumpy, which is brought about by rubbing too much on the edge, *i.e.* holding the handle of the tool too high.

If occasionally held up to the light, it may be seen whether it has been rubbed sufficiently, as the parts untouched will appear bright in contrast to the dull parts already worked upon. Again, if an arras, or rough edge, may be felt after rubbing, the tool will only require stropping to remove that and complete the process of whetting.

Stropping is the final touch. The tool is worked, as a barber does his razors, upon a piece of leather, buff for choice. Soldiers' old belts make excellent strops, which, for carving purposes, must be flexible, to fit the inside of the gouges. The leather must first be prepared upon one side by a mixture of crocus powder and tallow being well rubbed into its surface.

One practical demonstration, where possible, in sharpening tools would serve the student better than many pages of confusing instructions, clear only to the writer.

Tools become dull soon enough without any assistance from the worker, who by careless arrangement allows the edges to come in contact with each other.

The proper and safest position for tools upon the bench is when they scarcely touch each other, and placed with their edges towards the worker.

Of those used in this course, the **V** tool is at once the most awkward, "though but momentarily," and the most useful of the carver's set. Its use tends to develop the much-desired power to produce and appreciate good sweeping curves, either in abstract or actual form, and the importance of its general use cannot be overrated. In the holding of this tool, and in fact any other, it should not be gripped too firmly, for if it does not retard the flow of one's ideas through the tool to the material, it certainly cramps the flow of lines which those ideas suggest. Hold as near the sharp edge as convenient to work with, and sufficiently firm to prevent

TOOLS. 27

slipping; it may be pushed, or, by means of a mallet, it may be forced along the line of design, a difficulty in using presenting itself only when the worker allows it to become embedded in the wood. The top corners, $\overset{A\ B}{V}$, should always be in view. The thickness of line producible by this tool depends entirely upon the angle at which it is held: if well up at the handle, the line may be as deep as the section of the tool.

It is very necessary to acquire early a thorough knowledge and control of this particular tool, as, until one is in that happy position, it seems to have a most undesirable knack of going in any but the right direction, and its possibilities for use when under control, are more than the original intention of its maker. Use it whenever possible, even to removing as much ground as convenient to get at. Main lines and stems so produced are far more beautiful than those obtained by careful setting-in with gouge and chisel; by no other means can the subtle curves of stems, etc., so characteristic in nature, be produced so well.

The other tools, being gouges of different curvatures, call for no further comment. It matters little which side or size is used, so long as it effects the object in view; 9 and 10 are additional useful tools, the latter being called a bent gouge, or grounding-out tool.

Tools, like horses, seem to know their drivers, and require forcing to do their work; let them be as servants, means to an end. Lastly, treat them as friends, so that, understanding them better, you will not ignore the many new cuts or ideas they so often suggest. Dexterity being the outcome of practice, and there being no royal road, are facts especially applicable to the learning of wood-carving.

WOOD

BEST pine-wood is suggested for all exercises, except Figs. XXXI.–XXXVII., not entirely by reason of its easy-cutting qualities, and the quick results obtainable, so dear to the beginner, but partly because students will only learn by experience that the material they are to use has a nature requiring a certain amount of study or consideration. This particular wood, by virtue of its freeness in the grain, liability to split, is obviously best suited for the purpose. The expert, knowing his material, and therefore its limitations, can produce exactly his desired effect; the average student, on the other hand, begins by worrying it away, with a rough and rugged result.

At every point a little observation and thought will suggest the way wood should be treated; it resents tearing or dragging away, and seems to appreciate proper—*i.e.* firm—cutting. Whenever presenting a rough appearance, it is suggesting a *reverse* or sideways treatment of cutting. When cutting accurately, the student at once feels every assurance of the fact.

In cutting, he should try to produce a low whistling sound, by slightly curving the tool from side to side, when possible, in its progress forward. Perfect smoothness of finish is not required in the initial stages, as it is the outcome of time and practice only. To expect a beginner to master his material and tools on the first two or three models is surely too much, unless he already possesses some knowledge of material. When the finish is produced by means of a plane, this may be possible, for if the material will not be cut clean one way, it is but a matter of turning it about. In carving, every tool-cut produces its own plane, more or less; and as sand-paper is absolutely forbidden, some allowance must be made; in fact, tool-marks improve the general effect.

It does not necessarily follow that the experienced wood-worker has every advantage over the beginner.

Whilst admitting that dexterity comes of careful practice, which, in its turn, indicates command of the means whereby we seek to express ourselves, yet high finish should not be obtained at the expense of frittering away a student's enthusiasm.

Given an advanced copy, a student may worry the wood away in obtaining his desired forms; yet an intelligent appeal to complete his success, by carefully finishing the edges, etc., will have more effect than several lessons devoted to grounding out, with no tangible purpose in view. Chip-cutting *is* a form of carving which may be said to cultivate precision and care ; but this means of cultivating precision and care has two disadvantages : 1st. The majority of cuts are upon the slant, which, by the way, are those cuts least demanding for their production any special consideration of the material, therefore of little practical use in relief work, especially as a preparatory step. Granting, for the labour expended, very effective work, apparently, may be produced, yet the habit acquired for niggling far outweighs any such advantages of being attractive, effective, etc. 2nd. The excessive use of compass and rule creates an evil by training hand and eye to a dexterity in conforming to, and reliance upon, artificially-produced curves, which become less interesting as they approach perfection in their execution.

The difference between South Sea Islanders' work and the best modern chip work is easily seen—in the former examples much more freedom is displayed. The same thing is noticeable in the early Gothic tracery—the subtle curves of which are not those produced by the compass and stamped with its accurate characteristics. The drawing and writing of the nineteenth-century children very clearly shows the rigid grip they have of the unsympathetic means—" pen and pencil "—whereby they express themselves. The suggestiveness of the hard pen or pencil line is too slight to appeal to them; but substitute those means for another—" the supple brush"—and they have within their fingers a power—a means for expressing feeling, thought, life—a freedom unlimited in possibilities.

Too many are the ways and means for dwarfing the imaginative plant, by giving its co-partner in design, "construction," an undue share of attention. The eye, and also the hand, being very sensitive, promptly repay any want of confidence by acting in accordance with estimated worth. Precision and care are very desirable features, but their early cultivation in carving should not be too much insisted upon.

Each model has been produced by cuts most easy to obtain in the material, and, if followed carefully, a high standard of *technique* may be obtained, but at the expense of creating copyists. If the student is to give his ideas full play, his efforts must not be restricted too much. It is quite possible to produce such beautiful forms as may require the experience of a professional to complete technically. If this should be the outcome of the freedom advocated, then the student should be encouraged, not compelled, to see beauty in subtle forms, as in the laurel leaf, in contradistinction to the developed hart's tongue fern.

Exercises XXXI.–XXXVII., and remaining illustrations, may be worked in oak, alder, lime, kauri-pine, walnut, or mahogany; oak for preference.

HOLDING THE WORK

STUDENTS must not underrate the importance of making their work secure before beginning operations. The majority of accidents may be traceable to this want of care. The simplest methods, and all-sufficient for this course, are shown in the illustration of a block held firm by means of clips, which may be made of iron or wood. Two such clips are required, and may be fixed as follows: At A the clip is driven into the edge of the block to be carved, at B and C it rests upon the top surface. G cramps are useful where screw-holes may not be put in the bench-tops.

Another method, the simplicity of which may recommend itself, is that of gluing

PLAN FOR HOLDING WORK.

the block to be carved on to a larger piece of wood. If paper is put between, the separation, by means of inserting a chisel, becomes an easy matter. First glue the paper down upon the larger piece of wood; this done, glue about one inch round the edges of paper, sufficient to hold the edges of the block, not all over; then hold the block until the glue has set.

WORKING DIRECTIONS

PLATE I.

MATERIALS required: Block of pine-wood $7\frac{1}{2}'' \times 6'' \times 1''$; sheet of carbon or transfer paper, and drawing-pins.

Having prepared the drawing—which should be sketched, not traced, from the working drawing, Fig. I.—to occupy the block, fix it with pins upon the wood, with carbon paper between, then trace carefully over the lines with a hard pencil, and the drawing will be reproduced upon the wood.

On reference to Fig. I., it will be seen that the wood about the leaf form has been removed to a certain depth. As a guide for the depth, mark along the edge of the wood to be operated upon a line,

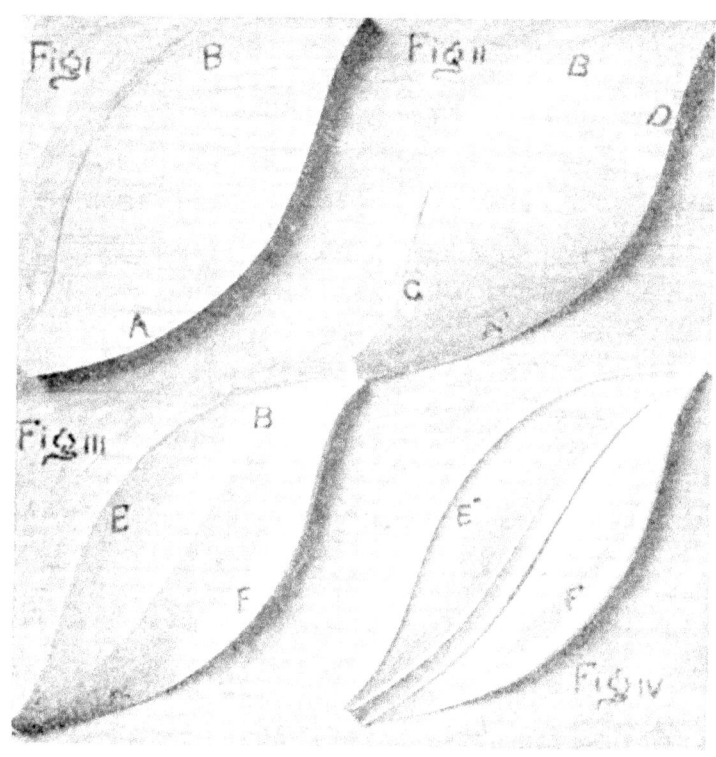

PLATE I.

say $\frac{3}{4}''$ down from the face; this depth will be understood as applying to Figs. I.–XXX., and XXXIV.–XXXVII. inclusive; with **V** tool cut round the outline of design, but not quite up to it. Then take gouge No. 1, and with it remove as much of the spare wood about the design as possible. This done, proceed to **trim** or **pare** the edges perpendicular to the ground, but this time quite up to the lines.

The technical terms for these processes are "grounding out and setting in," the lower level being called background. It is very important that this should be done fairly accurately in the early stages of the work, as success is partly measured by the uniformity of ground depth, and the sharp, square-down treatment of the edges, which should be neither ragged nor uneven, a result brought about by half cutting the edges down, and then dragging or gnawing the remainder of the wood away. A moment's reflection will suggest the remedy when the student finds his work rough and untidy at this point.

The ground must show that it has been cut with tools, not as though it had been first planed up perfectly smooth, and then the carving glued down upon it. Tool marks are not bits of wood in and about the design, as at *A*, Fig. xxxii., and *B*, Fig. xxxiii. Stamping, as generally practised, is often but a means to disguise careless work. The claim in its favour of clearly defining the design is weak. The ground and carving being one, why separate by suggesting that the carving had been fret-cut in the first instance, and fixed upon a different texture to its own?

The art of wood-carving, briefly, is the

creation of beautiful forms, and this may be illustrated upon the block of wood now prepared and standing up above the background. (Fig. I.) For the purpose of this book a beautiful form denotes a true, pleasing curved surface. With gouge No. 1 carefully round the edge at any part of the leaf, form Fig. I., say point *A*. See that the curve is gradual and quite down to the ground, so that as much flat surface as possible may be avoided.

The characteristic features of good wood-carving are contrast and variety. Contrast may be obtained by keeping the parts as high as possible directly opposite those taken down, as at *C* high, at *A* low; at *B* low, and *D* high, thus producing light and shade with the material. Variety may be introduced by treating the opposite side *B* as at *A*. Fig. II. illustrates the carrying out of this form-creation. Variety and contrasts of form will make the work look generally lumpy unless connected; so that to these two important principles must be added continuity, the merging of one form into another, as at Fig. III. In this manner a good, pleasing general effect is secured by connecting the created forms at *A* and *B* by means of tool 1, one decided sweep or throw from end to end.

The successful connection of these forms or ideas being so important, the stepping outside of the subject for further illustrations to emphasise its importance is fully justified. So long as single keys are struck upon the piano, "the sound emitted being termed for the purpose, ideas," all may be well; touch a group, and a discord or harmony may be there. In the first instance, to give individual attention is possible; in the second, lack of sympathy of tone causes each note to claim attention at one and the same time; in the third instance, they seem to run one into the other, the exact joint being imperceptible. This continuity applies to colour, book-writing, etc.; thus carving may be a book, a scheme of colour, a piece of music. As harmony is to the ear, colour to the eye, books to the mind, so is carving to the sense of love for the beautiful. If the carver has failed to endow his work with a continuity of thought, he has yet much to learn.

The student will do well to remember that it is not a matter of abundance of form, but just sufficient and well connected, to render the flat surface more pleasing, or more interesting to himself at least.

Returning to Fig. III., the form may be made more interesting by the addition of a conventional stem, the **V** tool only being used for the purpose. This done, slightly hollow the same; for if rounded it would look heavy, and if cut narrow, weak. At *E* and *F* an improvement may be made by the use of a quicker gouge, say No. 2 or No. 3.

These additions are suggested to draw attention to the relative uses of tools referred to, and more clearly to define already existing cuts.

Experience, the outcome of observation, will develop the tastes for adding successfully these final touches, which, although not necessary, yet impart to the work a crispness, lightness, not otherwise obtainable. From underneath, at the points standing highest above the ground, the wood may be cut away, the object of this being to produce a further light effect in the work, and not to show how far under or how thin and feathery the edges may be cut. In fact, the latter should invariably be bevelled about $\frac{1}{32}$ of an inch thick.

The technical term for this operation is "under-cutting," and it is important that no "under-cutting" be done until the completion of the top surface; as before stated, it is but a means to improve existing work. The completed exercise, Fig. IV., should, throughout its development, be influenced by the idea that the flat, smooth surface of Fig. I., produced by a soulless machine, demands a treatment that shall please the artistic senses. To do this, the most must be made of the wood projecting above the ground, so that if one part is kept full up, there can be no reason why corresponding parts may not be as low as possible—in fact, merging into the ground.

In the majority of instances, this half-expression of thought, or purpose, is the actual cause of students feeling that something is wrong with their work; and too often as a consequence they erect their own stumbling-block, *i.e.* "FEAR TO SPOIL," fear to take off too much wood.

In working to a copy this may be possible; but in utilizing slips which may be accidental cuts or pieces broken off, is found one of the secrets of success, *i.e.* twisting the unsatisfactory part into something else. Dictate a cut, and a check is placed upon the much-wished-for freedom; encourage the development of these slips, and confidence, self-reliance, is fostered. Often the developed slip, the apparently ruined corner, becomes the most honoured cut in the piece of work. Wood being cheap enough, begin your work boldly, not in a niggling manner, always applying the following tests :—

1. Are the forms or ideas properly carried out?

2. Are the forms or ideas properly connected?

3. Is the outline true?

4. Is the detail sufficient or too little, or, as often, too much.

PLATE II.

Figs. v.–vii. Material required, two pine-wood blocks $7\frac{1}{2}'' \times 6'' \times 1''$.

Mark design as already suggested, each occupying a block.

Carefully ground out with gouge No. 1, not forgetting to take the **V** tool round, but not quite up to the lines as a first step. This done, cut the edges clean, and quite up to the lines.

With gouge No. 1 round the end *A*, Fig. v.

Round down to ground at *E*, as *A* or *B*, Fig. II.

Connect *E* to *A*, as *A* to *B*, Fig. III.; this will produce Fig. VI.

Cut ends *B*, Fig. V., and complete as *B*, Fig. VI.

Bevel the edges.

Undercut.

Figs. VII., VIII. Round at I.

Remove a little of material at *G*, to facilitate completion of turnover I.

Cut ends *H*, as *B*, Fig. V.

Round to ground at *C*.

Connect *C* to *G*, as *A* to *B*, Fig. III.

Complete ends *H*, as Fig. VIII.

Bevel edges.

Undercut.

Remarks.—The exercises Plate I. show how pleasing forms may be created. In these two exercises (Plate II.) we apply that power in producing at given points a

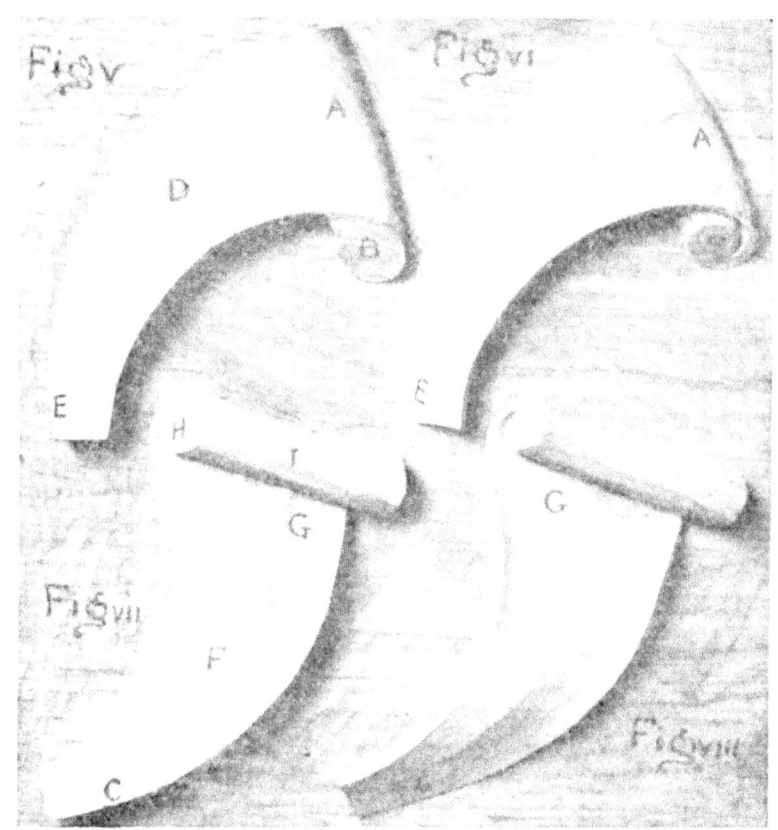

PLATE II.

definite idea. Such ideas may be taken from nature, casts, or photos. If a student is capable of creating the elementary forms as in Figs. I.–IV., it may be safely presumed that he is able to combine these forms at given points, producing a given idea : in this instance a scroll or roll of paper. Knowing that a scroll must be round, a standard is fixed for his guidance. Nothing less than a truly rounded coil will be satisfactory, otherwise the purpose or thought is only half expressed.

This done, a quantity of material, *D*, *F*, remains for further treatment. Apply Fig. II. and its lesson. Seeing that any other form than a flat surface will look more interesting, it matters little which part is thrown down; *C* and *E* are suggested. Thus we obtain three forms or ideas, *E A B*, Fig. VI., *C G I*, Fig. VIII., and these separate forms require continuity to complete their success, this being brought about as suggested at Fig. III.

PLATE III.

Material: Two or four blocks of pine-wood $7\frac{1}{2}'' \times 6'' \times 1''$.

Sketch design upon the wood, in each instance with one clear outline, as Figs. IX. and XI.

Ground out.

Create first form at *A*, then *B*, afterwards *C*, Fig. IX.

Create first form at *D*, then *E*, afterwards *F*, Fig. XI.

Figs. IX.–X. and XI.–XII. have the same forms.

Connect these three forms, *i.e.* merge one into another.

The surface of Fig. IX. is then treated, as per illustration, with tools 1 and 4.

PLATE III.

Figs. x. and xii. have had their edges broken and surface treated with gouges 2 and 4 ; Fig. xi. the surface treated with gouges 1, 2, 4 ; Fig. xii. edges and surface treated with gouge No. 2. It will be noticed that the small corners are rounded off; also notice the effects gained by varying the width of bevel on the edges.

Undercut.

Remarks.—As every leaf upon the tree varies in form, so may those in carving; yet nothing less than a beautiful form "completed" must be the basis of operation, and it cannot be too often repeated —form first, details afterwards.

Make more interesting by addition of lines, stems, &c., but not at the cost of destroying the original form in the least degree. The additional lines, stems, cuts, etc., must tend to radiate from or to the centre, and, if possible, express the contour of the form.

In this exercise the student is given scope for experimenting as to the relative value of different tools. The result of experimenting will be more pleasing than the working of Fig. IV.

PLATE IV.

Materials: Block of pine-wood $7\frac{1}{2}'' \times 6'' \times 1''$.

Mark design upon the wood.

Take **V** tool round the lines as before, then ground out.

Free the leaf-form *A* by cutting some of the wood away, as at *B B*.

Treat the centre in its various stages like Fig. IV. has been done.

Give to the side leaves a little more throw or form, as at *C C*.

Complete by merging the forms thus

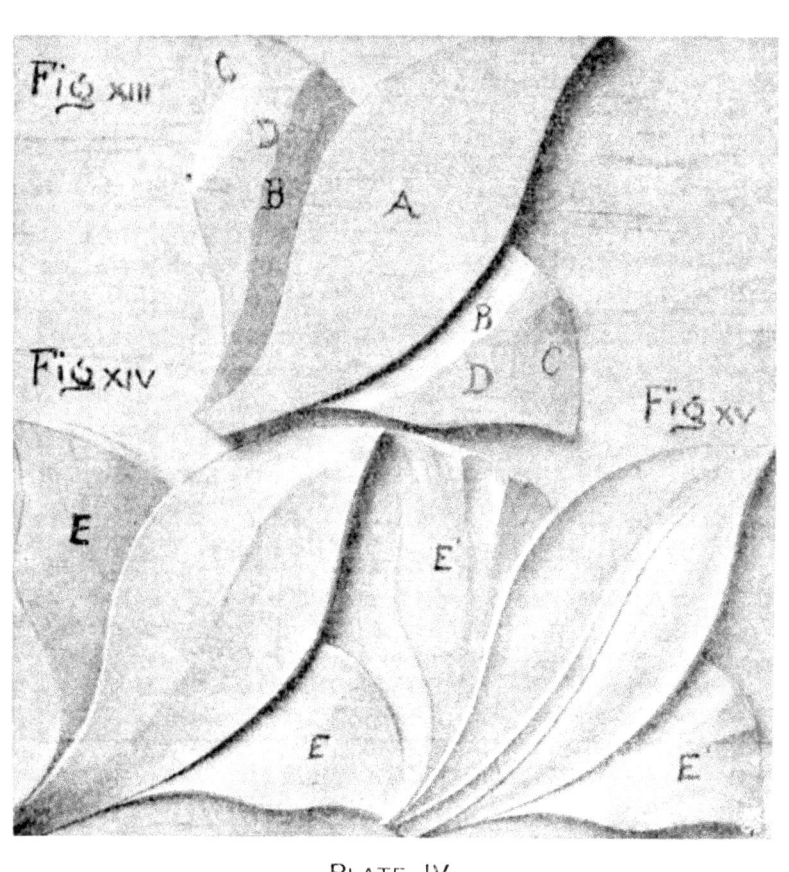

PLATE IV.

produced, *C D B*, as shown at *E E*, Fig. XIV.

Playfully treat the surface, as shown in Figs. IX.–XII.

Bevel the edges, and undercut.

Remarks.—The value of this exercise is the combination of previous work, but of much more in importance is it one for developing concentration of thought upon a given feature in a design. Generally speaking, the best plan to adopt in working any design is to single out its main line or feature, making that successful first, from a form point of view, afterwards paying heed to the smaller features. The average student is wanting in method, and very often he finds himself going over his work many times with no appreciable result. He is too fond of touching it up, putting in a cut here and there, and all over the panel, thus expressing want of continuity in method of working, finishing, etc.

The royal road to finishing carved work is none other than taking up one tool, after the main features have been roughed in or "boasted," and with it finish every cut it may be capable of doing, putting it down, only to take up another, the next in usefulness, and so on. This method, perhaps, requires more self-control than the amateur is capable of, because the temptation is very great to pick up a tool just to take out one little bit.

The next best method is to begin at the root of the design, and thrash out its main features; afterwards complete the smaller features, etc.

PLATE V.

Figs. XVI., XVII. Material: Pine-wood, $6'' \times 6'' \times 1''$.

Sketch design upon the wood, and as large as it will allow.

Ground out.

With gouge No. 2 produce cut *A B A*, taking notice that it begins close to the ground at *A*, rising gradually to *B*, and then falling to *A*.

The flat surfaces, *C D*, require connecting to this hollow thus created, which is done by softening off the ridge between them and the cut *A B A*.

Bevel the edges and undercut.

Figs. XVIII., XIX. Material, $7\frac{1}{2}'' \times 7\frac{1}{2}'' \times 1''$.

The same cuts as in last exercise, Fig. XVI.

By the addition at each corner, *H H*, to above design (Fig. XVI.) a different effect is produced.

The gouge-cut *E F G*, a repeat of cut *A B A*, has been continued or run through *H H H*, as at *I I I*.

Remarks.—This scroll is very useful as a detail for building up designs; and as its success in drawing depends upon its truth in curvature, so is a true decided sweep-cut none the less important in its carving. If the main line, or cut, of a design suggests weakness, no amount of finish will compensate for the defect. The well-developed skeleton of the human form—however ill-clothed with beautiful details of muscles, etc.—is preferable to the well-clothed but deformed skeleton, from a designer's standpoint.

These two exercises (Figs. XVI.–XVIII.) give further scope for the exercise of a student's taste, in that he may add touches of improvement wherever his fancy suggests an opportunity.

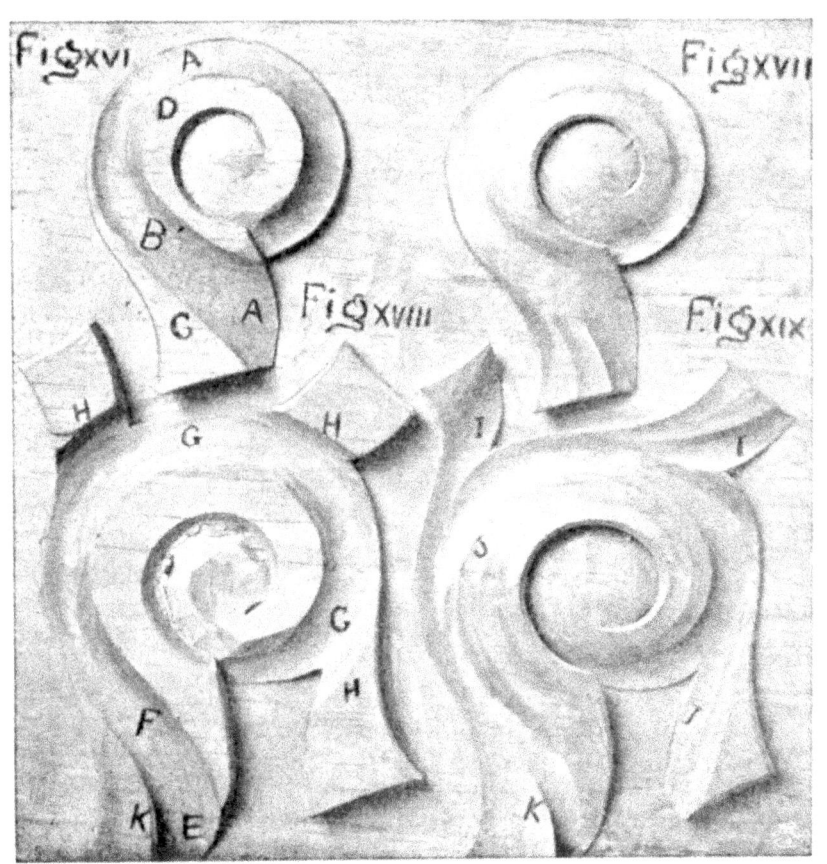

PLATE V.

Upon reference to the illustrations, Figs. XVII. and XIX., it will be noticed that some of the hard lines in Figs. XVI. and XVIII. have been retained, but so modified as to give a pleasing effect. Their retention depends upon the student's taste, so toning them down as to appear part of the form. When not too obtrusive, these lines improve the appearance of the work; but beware of too many. It is not by covering the work with lines and cuts that poor forms are disguised; in fact, such treatment emphasises its weakness in that respect. A good form creates its own safeguard, if the student will but listen to its appeal for just sufficient detail to make it look interesting, and no more.

Notice that the lines are not continuous, and points *K I I I* give you various treatments as finishes, each varying in strength of tool marks.

PLATE VI.

Figs. XX.–XXII. Material: Pine-wood, $7\frac{1}{2}'' \times 6'' \times 1''$.

Sketch design upon wood, and as large as it will allow.

Take **V** tool round the lines, then ground out.

Free the centre *A* by cutting the material away at *S S*.

Treat each one exactly as Figs. VI. and VIII.

Remarks. — As Plate IV. is to Plate I., so is this Plate VI. to Plate II.

The same purpose is served and the same instructions as for Plate IV.

Figs. XXIII., XXIV. These are details for future use.

Material: Pine-wood, $6'' \times 6'' \times 1''$.

With gouge No. 2, one cut from *I*, to *G*, to *H*.

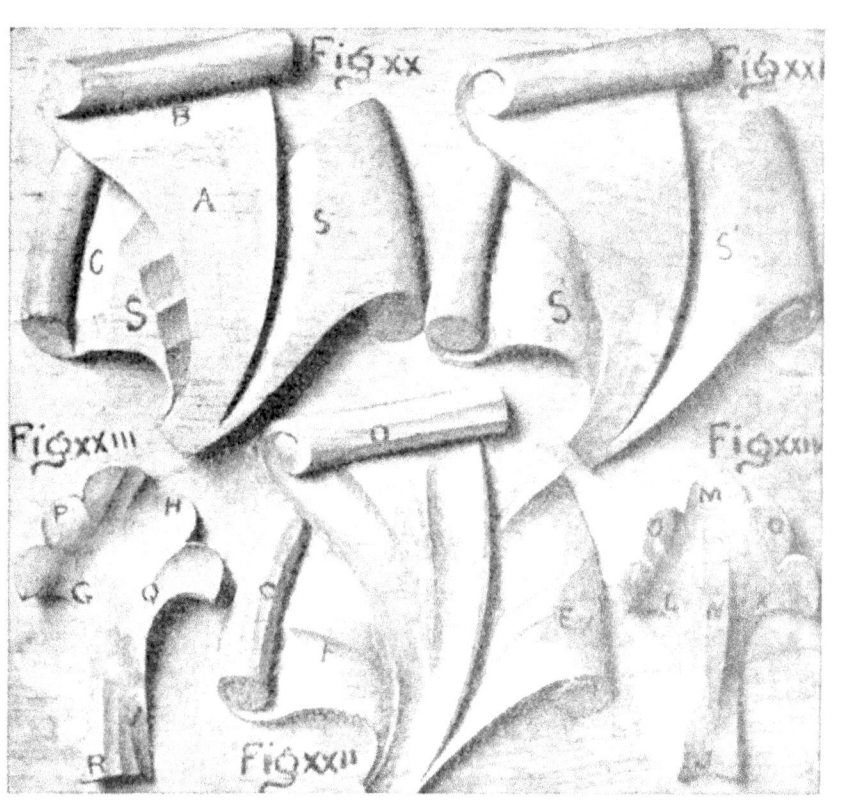

PLATE VI.

WORKING DIRECTIONS. 73

With gouge No. 2, one cut from *J*, to *K*, to *M*.

With gouge No. 2, one cut from *J*, to *L*, to *M*.

Notice the contrast: down at *I G H*, *J L M K*, and high at *R P Q N O*. Also notice that the touches upon the prominent parts are only sufficient for the purpose; their continuation, from a technique point of view, would be troublesome at least, with no corresponding advantage to the general effect, if any at all.

PLATE VII.

Material: Pine-wood, $6'' \times 6'' \times 1''$.

Sketch and ground out design as large as wood allows.

Fig. xxv. The idea suggested is that of interlacing.

A A is lowered to pass underneath *C*; *B* and *D* under *A*.

Remarks.—In Figs. xxv. and xxvi. may

be seen the line dividing the good and indifferent worker. In the former, the indifferent mechanical worker is seen. In the latter may be seen the sympathetic worker and his treatment of the same design. The interlacing of ornament goes far to make it interesting, and what holds good in flat also holds good in modelled ornament. This principle is involved in this exercise, *i.e.* the creation of beautiful forms subject to others in contact.

To the mechanical interlacing of Fig. xxv. has been added the principle evolved in Fig. II. Each form is taken as Fig. I., and treated as Figs. II., III.; down at GH, up, as a contrast, gradually from G to I, the same at MM, KL. The surfaces of these twisting forms are treated more or less as suggested on Plate III., central lines being most in evidence.

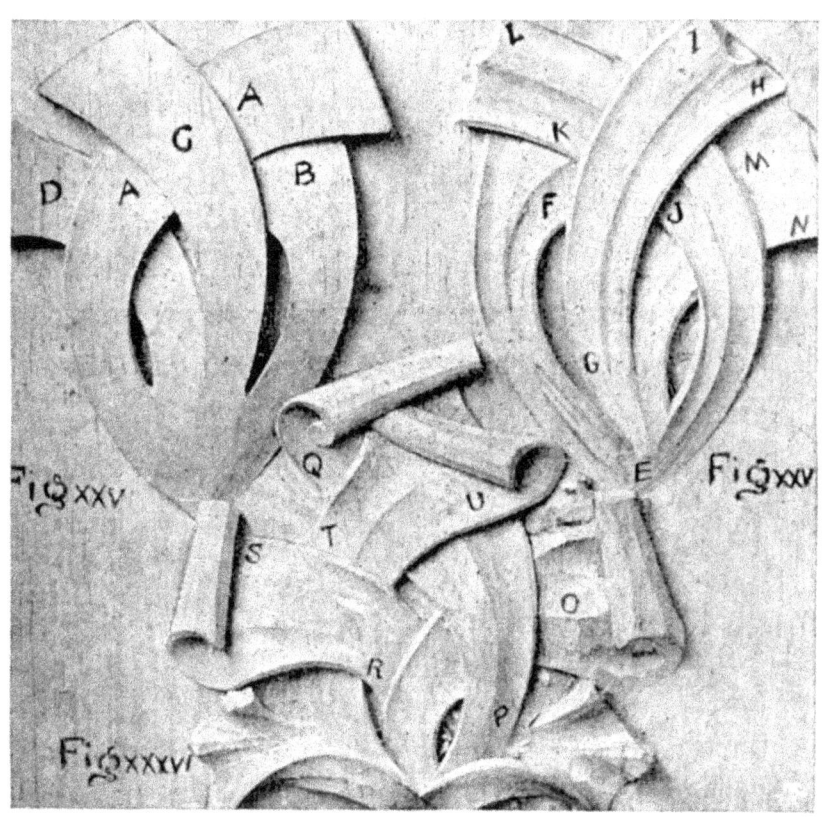

PLATE VII.

Notice the combination of hollow and round cuts on the surface of the forms; not too much of each feature, as it is quite possible to completely disguise those forms beyond recognition, and this is not the purpose of details; notice also the bevelled edges, the continuity of forms in the interlace of the same, the throw or spirit of the work. Undercut.

Fig. XXXVI. is a combination of Fig. XXVI., to which is added open scrolls, as on Plate II. The outer side of example being unfinished, suggests method of working.

PLATE VIII.

Wood—$7\frac{1}{2}'' \times 6'' \times 1''$—pine, alder, or lime.

Fig. XXVII. Ground out.

With tool No 2 take one sweep cut, as at B.

Lower the wood at A, with opposite side L as high as the wood will allow; contrast.

Free the corner at *D*, keeping the outer edge well up, as a contrast to part going under at *A*.

Merge cut *B* into *C*, as in *B D*, Figs. XVI.–XIX.

With same gouge, cuts *F* and *G* may be produced.

Fig. XXVIII. Undercut.

Fig. XXIX. Wood, $7'' \times 5'' \times 1''$.

The main stem is down at *J H I*, with opposite sides contrasting.

From *J*, gradually rising to *K*.

Fig. XXX. Double arrangement of Fig. XXVIII. Wood, $8'' \times 6'' \times 1''$.

Remarks. — These examples are self-explanatory, showing, as they do, how leaves and stems may break away from each other.

Fig. XXVII. is a broad stem *A*, half clothed with a leaf. Leaves, being details, must

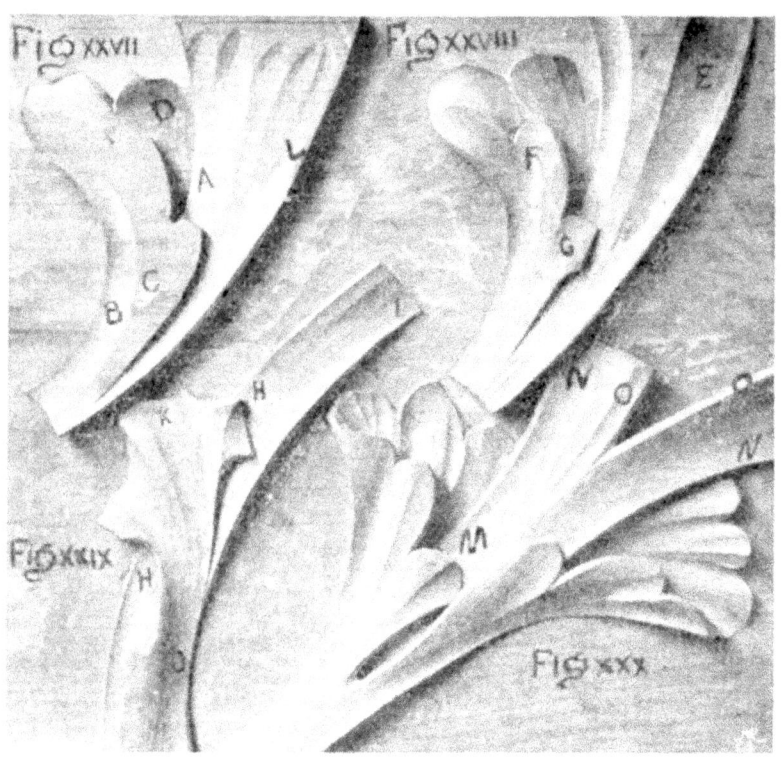

PLATE VIII.

partake of the same form at their junction with the stem, which carries the design onward, *i.e.* gradually springing away from the stem, unless when specially articulated.

Fig. XXVIII. The forms are completed, and the play of tools, as seen on Plate III., applied, the main stem being taken down at E, as a contrast to L, which projects to the full extent of material.

Fig. XXIX. shows stem bending and twisting about, a leaf thrown over, and partaking of that same twist as at JK.

Fig. XXX. shows a double arrangement of Fig. XXVII., also the junction of two stems. Notice the throw of same, down at M and N, up at O.

PLATE IX.

Wood — $12'' \times 12'' \times {}^5/_8''$ — walnut, alder, kauri-pine; the latter for preference.

This is a combination of all previous exercises.

The main stem is Fig. XVIII. opened out and clothed; the corner pieces, by the application of details (Plate VIII.), become leaf forms, which in themselves are groups or compounds of smaller leaves (Fig. IV).

The border, or working within a margin, is first introduced here. There is no objection to it being cut straight down to the ground at the margin line, other than its suggestiveness of too much "frame." The ground, if curved, and thereby brought up to the surface, certainly looks better than the former treatment.

PLATE IX.

Proceed as before with **V** tool, removing as much ground $\frac{3}{8}''$ deep as convenient with same tool; whilst admitting that tool 2 will do this quicker, yet it affords an opportunity for further practice. This done, trim up the lines by carefully setting in, cutting firmly down to the depth required. Begin with tool 1 wherever it will go, then tool 6, and so on, until the lines of the design are clearly defined. Use the largest tools where possible for cleaning up the ground. In places where the design passes over other portions, it is not necessary to set in other than deep enough to retain the lines of pattern.

Begin with the main feature first—the stem—and, in the cutting, notice that the forms have been produced by a cut with tool No. 2, taken along the back or outside edge of the scroll or main stem. This cut is varied by being down to the ground at *A C E G*, gradually rising in each instance to *B D F H*. The inner edge of coil is fully up from beginning to end. Remove the wood at points *J*, suggesting its coming from underneath, remembering the necessary contrast at *K*. Reference to Plate VIII. will supply the other details for cutting.

PLATE X.

Wood — $12'' \times 7\frac{1}{2}'' \times {}^5/_8''$ — kauri, walnut, oak.

Side *A* is merely roughed in or boasted, tool No. 1 being much in evidence.

Notice that *C* and *D* is taken down, and the remainder of centre softened into it. Being self explanatory, calls for no further comment, other than no motive as a scroll is so useful to practise upon for the production of good sweeping cuts.

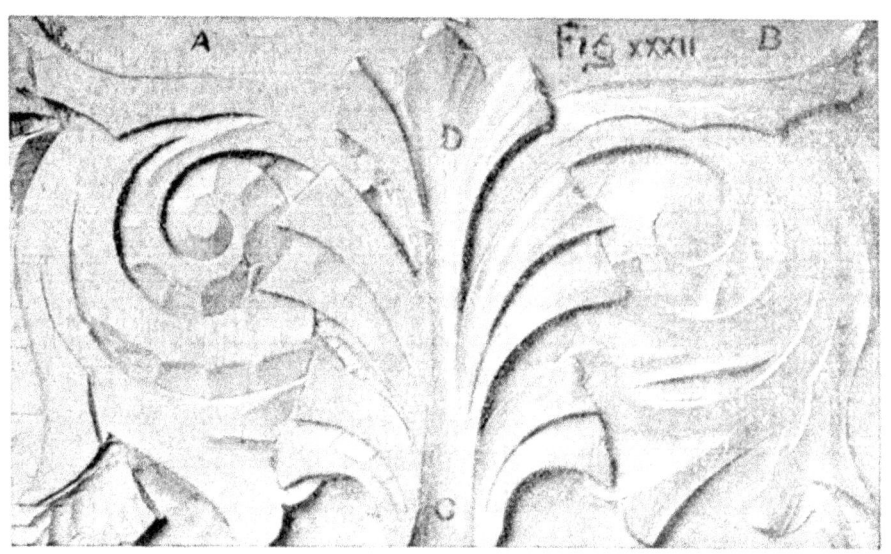

PLATE X

PLATE XI.

PLATE XI.

Wood—$12'' \times 12'' \times {}^5/_8''$—oak.

Portion at *A* is completed.

At *B* may be seen the earlier stage of boasting out the design preparatory to finishing.

Notice points at *D* are down, and points at *C* up.

The design is built up of details in combination; the main stem, Fig. XXVI., lengthened with foliated ends, as Figs. XXIII.–XXIV. Fig. XXX. in evidence at the root of pattern.

PLATE XII.

Figs. XXXIV.–XXXV.—wood, $9'' \times 6'' \times 1''$.

Fig. XXXVII., $9'' \times 9'' \times 1''$. Oak wood.

More elaborate details, singly and in compound, form Fig. XXXVII.

The additional designs found in the set of working drawings may be worked as the student feels inclined to do: remembering, as he must, that merely laying one piece of the design under another is not all. The designer fixes those conditions. The student must accept them, and set about to create his beautiful forms under the given circumstances of line arrangement.

Fig. XXXVI. See Plate VII.

The conventional square leaf-forms clothing the stems are but suggestions. Within those outlines may be sketched and cut such elaborate details as the acanthus foliage, etc.

PLATE XII.

PLYMOUTH :
WILLIAM BRENDON AND SON,
PRINTERS.

Manual Training Tool Co.

<u>CARVER STREET,</u> **SHEFFIELD.**

CARVING TOOLS. *All Patterns.*

ILLUSTRATED LIST ON APPLICATION.

(MR. PHILLIPS' SET.)

Mr. J. Phillips' Set of 10 Tools, sent out handled, ground, and specially sharpened, ready for use.

BOOK.—Mr. J. Phillips' "Course of Wood Carving," 3/6.
  CASTS for same:
    SET A.—First 7 Casts, **17/6**.
    SET B.—5 Advanced Casts, **15/-**.
  Shaded Working Drawings, SET of 16: Full Size of Casts, **5 -**.

PANELS.—24 Panels, to cover Phillips' Complete Course, in Pine, Alder, Kauri, and Oak.
  Wood well seasoned, and carefully planed.
  Any Size Panel to Order.

OBJECTS FOR CARVING.—Set of Objects for Carving in preparation, 20 Objects, including Mirror and Photo Frames, Brackets, Chair Backs, Bookshelves and Racks, Corner Cupboard, Coal Box, Table Top, etc.

CHIP CARVING. Set of 4 Tools, including **V** Tool, **2/6**.

GEM MALLET.—A handsome tool, round, polished head, **1/-**.

SLIPS.—Set of 4 Arkansas, **2/9**.

Cramps, Strops, Stones, Sharpening Paste, Small Grindstones, Carver's Clips, and Screws.

— CLASSES COMPLETELY FITTED FOR CARVING —
AND ALL KINDS OF MANUAL WORK.

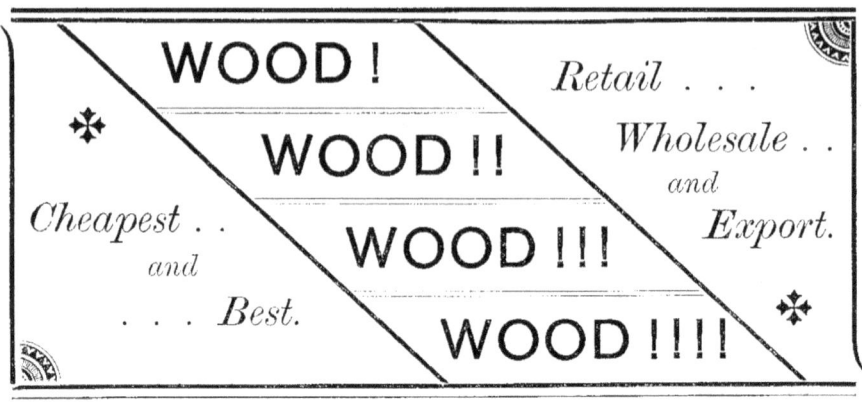

COBBETT & CO..
CASH TIMBER MERCHANTS,

| WRITE for PRICE LIST FREE. | 64 & 66, Virginia Road, Bethnal Green, LONDON, E. | PLANED FRETWOODS and PREPARED PANELS. |

AMERICAN BLACK WALNUT.   SATIN WALNUT.   FIGURED OAK.
YELLOW PINE.   PITCH PINE.   KAURI PINE.   CANARY WHITEWOOD.
RED WOOD.   MAHOGANY.   CANADIAN ASH.   POPLAR.

Picture-frame Mouldings.   **Gilt Slips and Backboards.**
Squares for Turning.

SPECIAL OFFER!

We will send FREE, on receipt of 3/-, SIX PREPARED PANELS—size, 12 in. by 12 in., prepared from prime $\frac{1}{4}$-inch of any of the following woods: Canary White Wood, Red Wood, Mahogany, Figured Oak, Black Walnut, Satin Walnut, and Canadian Ash.

Write for Price List to **COBBETT & CO.,**
66, Virginia Road, Bethnal Green, LONDON, E.

www.ingramcontent.com/pod-product-compliance
Lightning Source LLC
Chambersburg PA
CBHW051455290426
44109CB00016B/1769